Be awesome at online business

A handbook for succeeding on the web.

By Paul Jarvis

Copyright 2013 Paul Jarvis. All rights reserved.

Paul Jarvis   Author & Designer
Cheri Hanson   Editor
Lisa Lipka   Copyeditor

978-0991918638   ISBN

Feel free to take passages from this book and replicate them online or in print, but link back to pjrvs.com/book. If you want to use more than a few paragraphs, email paul@pjrvs.com. I built the Internet, so if you flat-out steal, I'll find out.

I also (might) exist outside of this book:

pjrvs.com   Web
@pjrvs   Twitter

Table of contents

Introduction	7
Start here	11
Defining your online business	19
Redefining your online business	25
Finding the right web designer	31
Getting an accurate project quote	37
Your project responsibilities	43
Design tips	47
Critiquing mockups	53
Making your website credible	59
Writing effective content	63
Ecommerce	69
Selling self-published products & services	73
Your launch responsibilities	81
Post-launch responsibilities	85
Promoting your website	91
Building a newsletter	97
Using social media	101
Conclusion	105
Companion book	109
Resources	111
About the author	115
Thanks	117

Designers have a dual duty; contractually to their clients and morally to the later users and recipients of their work.

— Hans Höger

Introduction

I am not a web ninja, Internet Jedi or even a marketing guru. But I have done web design (without a fancy job title) for fifteen years, helping hundreds of clients build awesome online businesses that are used by millions every year.

I've noticed that there's a lack of understanding about what's involved in creating, launching and maintaining an online business.

Simply having a website built isn't a business plan, nor is it enough to succeed. If you're opening a store in your neighborhood, you can't just hire an interior designer to make the inside look perfect, open the doors, and then watch people with wallets full of money flock in to buy things from you (followed promptly by a money fight on your private yacht).

This lack of understanding is my fault as a web designer and an online strategy person. Well, not mine specifically, but the fault of my industry as a whole. Anyone who helps others build online businesses, in any way, hasn't done the best job of teaching people what's involved, what they might be responsible for and what to do with the project when our jobs are finished.

That's where this book comes in. I want to teach you what you need to do in order to succeed online. Hell, I want you to *crush it*. Not because I have some altruistic vision for a perfect online world (holding hands and singing *kumbaya* over Skype), but because it benefits everyone involved (including people like me) when you do well.

I've gone into detail on the following pages about what you need to think about, plan for, actually do, and follow through with to make your online business work for you. You'll have a lot of homework, even if you've hired the best people to build your site.

If you've already got a website, I will help you learn some new ideas that could lead to greater success and exposure.

So read on friend—you've got an online business to launch (or re-launch).

Paul Jarvis

Start here

Why does this book exist?

Without getting all existential (why do any of us exist? maybe we're just a figment of this book's imagination?), I wrote this book to help you succeed online. Seriously. And that means there's lots of tough love and hard work involved.

I've spent so much time looking at the websites I've built and assessing what factors helped my clients to kick ass online. These super successful clients have a few key things in common:

1. They all have singular, clear and definable goals.

2. They've hired professionals who know their shit inside and out—from web design to photography to content strategy—and lean on them for their expertise (instead of just telling them how to do their jobs).

3. They don't attempt to do it all themselves.

4. They're masters of their crafts, so they aren't just passionate about what they do, they're also damn good at it.

5. They put the work in and know exactly what their audience wants and is willing to pay for. They spend time every single day maintaining relationships and building new ones in the online places that they know will net the best results.

6. They're badass motherfuckers who people actually listen to, respect and get value from. The 'making money' part comes as a natural progression after accomplishing all those things.

This book is also totally self-serving for every professional involved in building other people's online businesses. We all look good when our clients do well. They tell others, they come back for more work, and sometimes they invite us to pool parties on their private yachts (this hasn't actually happened to me, but one day...).

Why should I listen to you?

You don't have to, and I encourage you to question everything. Nothing in this book is a golden rule or a concrete system; if something like that existed, every website would be a success. It's more advice and ideas to ponder. You can ignore or disregard what I've laid out if it doesn't make sense to you. Just think about it first (which is really all I ask). I've built websites for a long time and I've measurably helped clients to reach their goals. This book is filled with what I've figured out from doing that work for well over a decade.

I've learned from both my own and my clients' successes (do you really learn from mistakes?) and summed up the ideas and tactics I've seen that actually work. But even at the time of writing this, I'm still constantly learning, refining, exploring and researching everything I talk about. The web evolves, and we all have to evolve with it, if we want to do well.

What's an online business?

I hate to break it to you, but every business is an online business. From a local vegan cupcake shop to a life coach to a professional kazoo player—every business exists in some way on the Internet. It can be as simple as a business listing on Google, to a full website and social media presence. Even if you don't think your business exists online, it probably does—in the form of reviews or listings on a search engine, social media site or business association website. So the advice and notes in this book apply to all businesses, not just super-nerdy tech ones that exist only online and sell digital products.

What if I already have an online business?

There's always room for improvement, right? Audit yourself and how your business works. Is it time for a redesign? A new project? More social media usage or blogging? Every topic in this book applies equally to existing businesses as it does to new ones. The minute you stop adapting to meet changing business needs is the minute your business isn't as successful as it could be.

What's a web designer?

For the purpose of the book and using a single term for clarity, I've chosen web designer. It can be applied to a single person or swapped out to mean web design company, agency or online collective. It should never mean 'my cousin who updated his Tumblr theme.'

Web designers think about programming, best web practices and functionality (plus, obviously, the visual stuff). If you think you can hire someone to design your website and later find some else to program it, you're leaving yourself open for massive problems. What if the design can't be easily programmed? What if it technically just won't work in code? What if it can't scale to mobile devices or doesn't fit how the ecommerce platform works? Never separate design and programming on a web project. Ever.

You should look for a web designer that can either a) fully design and program your website or b) always works with the same programmers to fill in the services they don't provide.

Why is less actually more?

Most people who know me know my penchant for minimalism (in web design, in furniture, in my lack of a robust wardrobe...). This isn't just because I fundamentally hate being a vapid consumer, but stems more from the time I've spent thinking about how complex all our lives have become.

There's so much noise competing for our focus and attention. We face constant distractions (from advertisements to notifications on our cell phones anytime anyone 'likes' anything we've posted). The noise is almost deafening.

This book is filled with suggestions about how to do less and focus more. But why is this important, and why is it a good business decision?

One of the most valuable skills anyone can have is to take a complex concept and boil it down into easy-to-understand terms. It's easy to have lots of words, lots of products, lots of everything. But then how does an audience figure out what they need?

To stand out as an online business, you need to get your message across quickly and clearly. This requires focus. Simplicity doesn't mean removing features or services; it means distilling what's most important and explaining yourself as concisely as possible. People won't remember the 15 benefits of what you're selling, but they will remember one or two if they're supremely beneficial.

Even with this book, I've spent more time paring it down and removing unnecessary content than I have writing new content. I cut over 6,000 words from the first draft to the final version, because I want this to be a quick read that gets to the point, without any fluff.

Defining your online business

Before even thinking about a website, you need to think about your plan.

I'm not talking 'plan' like 'formal business plan' with pie charts and meaningless phrases like 'a customer focused, best of breed, turn-key solution with outstanding ROI based on expertise' (say that three times fast). I'm talking about figuring out what, exactly, you're going to be selling. What are your products and/or services? What will make people want to buy from you? What would make those people want to share what you're offering with others? What does your work do to help people or make their lives easier? What makes it valuable? How can you turn visitors to your online business into a sustainable and engaged community?

Your website won't earn money, but your business will. A website, even an awesome one, isn't a magical money tree. So before focusing on what your website will have or even be, figure out your business. Your website will slide naturally into place and the people you hire to help build it will have a much easier time if you're focused and clear about what it needs to do.

Know right now you're not going to make a lot of money through ads. For the most part, they pay almost nothing, even if you have a fairly well-visited website. Ads are ugly – and they aim to entice visitors away from your website and your offerings. For the most part, you also can't control which ads show up. So, you might be a vegan cookbook author and your ad network serves up an ad for bacon wrapped steak. Does that make sense? Didn't think so.

The other concept people sometimes bring up is creating 'passive income.' This is hogwash (since really, who washes a pig?). Stop reading websites that teach (or worse sell) the idea that you can do almost no work and continually make lots of money. Passive implies not doing anything and watching the cash roll in. Plant that money tree instead; it's more environmental. Either way, if you want to make money, you have to work hard at it. Constantly. Even if it's a product you create once and sell to many (like this book), you've still got to promote and market it to keep selling. Any business idea that seems like you can do next to nothing and still make a lot of money probably has serious flaws or isn't based in reality.

Once you've got your online business idea figured out (which is no small feat), think about the goals. How are you defining success (it might have nothing to do with cash-money)? What will you do to sustain it? The goal of your online business can be anything from increasing your exposure and authority on a topic (so you can later create a product) to selling 10,000 copies of your latest ebook (which deals with pig-washing etiquette). Your goals should be clear and easily summarized, since you'll apply them to every decision you make moving forward—from approving mockups to writing copy to tweeting.

How will you measure your goals? What indicators will show you if your business is succeeding or not? Anything from increased mailing list subscribers, to selling products/services, to getting a certain number of guest posts on high-traffic websites can apply—just make sure the goals are measurable and that you don't have very many of them. Be a fucking laser, so your site can be equally laser-focused. After all, when was the last time you did 10 or even five specific things on a website you visited?

With your goals in hand, you'll move into design, content and promotion with a specific reason for every decision that you make. The process will move along faster and the end result will be better.

Once the business ideas are clear, you can then start contacting people to help you build your idea. Try not to get overwhelmed with this step. Remember that every business started with a single idea, a single product and a first customer.

Ten questions to consider before starting your online business

1. What am I selling? Who is my audience, and why will they want to buy my stuff?

2. Will what I'm selling generate rave reviews and turn customers into sales and marketing people? If not, how can I improve their experience?

3. What are my business goals? What does a successful business mean to me?

4. How will this make money? How will it continue to make money?

5. What makes this idea unique? What problem does it solve and how does it help people? What value does this bring to others?

6. What about this makes me excited? How can I spread that excitement?

7. What professionals do I need to hire to make this happen? What will they be responsible for doing?

8. What is my budget (and if it's not realistic, can it change)?

9. What is my timeline for launch (and if it's not realistic, can it change)?

10. What do I want my business to be known for?

Redefining your online business

If you've already got an online business, you're ready to figure out what's working and what's not. Even the most successful online businesses need to stay current for continued success.

Technologies, systems and your customers' needs change. What's relevant now might not be next year. It's survival of the most adaptable, and you've got to continue to adapt to make your business work.

Redefining your online business should never be just a website redesign. You first have to make real business decisions that will focus the redesign.

Are your goals still the same? Read the previous chapter and fill in the worksheet. Do your answers match how your current website works? If not, what needs to happen to re-align them? Do you need new products or services?

You can also start by benchmarking your current performance. Look at your statistics to see how many people are visiting your site, how quickly they're leaving and what page they are leaving from. How many sales do you make, compared to how many views your sales page receives? If you can't figure this out, try surveying your existing clients to gauge what they like and dislike about your online business. This is invaluable data, since you're learning directly from people who give you money or read your site, rather than making random assumptions. You can ask them a few simple questions:

1. What's not working?

2. What do they wish you offered?

3. Do they think the website adequately reflects who you are and what your business does?

A redesign should have clear reasons to proceed—past the desire for a fresh look. Clarify what you'd like to see happen by setting specific goals. Then when you hire a web designer, you can communicate those new goals and incorporate them into the redesign.

How is your online business faring on social media? Do you get many leads from any social networks? Which ones, specifically? Perhaps it's time to focus and engage on the networks that are bringing you traffic and sales.

It's also extremely important to consider what currently performs well in your online business. What is being shared most often? Linked to the most? Purchased most often? Obviously those things shouldn't change significantly, but it might be worth creating similar content or offerings based on what's currently doing well for you.

It's never a bad idea to scope out the competition. What are they doing that you aren't? What are they succeeding at that you might not be? You never want to copy someone else, but you can use their successes and shortcomings to your advantage by doing better in either case.

The main goal of any website redesign should be to better serve your audience (above adding fancy new bells and whistles). So, figure out where you're failing to meet their needs with what you offer and work on that.

Nine questions to ask before redesigning your online business

1. What measurable data do I have that supports a reason to redesign or tweak my online business?

2. What are my goals for the redesign? How will I measure them?

3. How will this redesign better serve both my existing audience and a new potential audience?

4. Can I survey my existing audience or customers to get their perspective?

5. Do I need new products or services?

6. Do I need to update existing products, services or even my own skill-set to better serve my audience?

7. What is the competition doing that I'm not, and how can I do better?

8. How is my brand perceived? Is that perception accurate? Is it negative? If so, what can I do to change that view?

9. Are there new technologies or systems (new ecommerce software, new content management systems, new newsletter applications, etc.) I can use to better serve my audience or automate more of my workflow?

Finding the right web designer

I realize that maybe your cousin is a web designer who builds websites on the side. Or that your friend's brother in college once updated your Tumblr in exchange for a case of beer. Or that you can, quite easily, figure out web design, programming and Wordpress yourself, but you just haven't found the time.

Web designers hear these types of comments a lot (possibly second only to "make the logo bigger" on mockups). While there's nothing wrong with learning new things or having hobbies, for the love of whatever god you believe in, hire a professional to design and program your website. Professional, as in someone who does web design full-time, as a job that they get paid money to do, and has done so for a while.

How do you find the right professional web designer? Do you walk into a hip coffee shop and look for plaid shirts, tattooed fingers and Apple laptops? While that would probably work, it makes more sense to start by looking at websites you enjoy visiting, and that appear to have a good community and engaged following. Does it say at the bottom of the website who designed and programmed it? If not, send a brief email to the website's owner, asking who they used and if they were happy with their designer.

Make a shortlist of designers (two or three) you want to work with (from looking at those sites you like and asking who built them). What are their portfolios like? Can you get behind the tone, aesthetics and presentation of their own websites and other websites they've done? Are their project sizes (features, functions, what the site does, etc.) similar in scope to yours?

Contact these web designers and actually talk to them on the phone (old school, I know). You want to make sure you understand how they communicate, since they'll be responsible for visually communicating your online business. Do they talk in technical jargon or Star Trek references (although the latter could be a bonus)? Are they clear about what they can provide for you? What is their process?

Ask for references and actually contact them. Ask each reference what it was like to work with the web designer. Find out if they delivered on time, on budget, and if the client could honestly recommend them.

There's no industry standard for pricing a website. They can cost next to nothing to well into six figures. Since you already have a good idea of your budget, see what the designer's average project typically costs to determine if your budget fits into that range. If the two numbers are way off, it's best to find out early to avoid wasting anyone's time.

Chances are if you've found a web designer who's responsible for a popular website, they're fully booked for a little while. Most good web designers are slammed (my own schedule books months in advance). So find out when they could start a project with you and how long projects typically take. There's so much you can do before a project starts, and waiting a while gives you a chance to do your own homework (see chapter title *Your project responsibilities*).

Be prepared to adjust time and money if none of the professionals you want to hire can work with your budget or timeline. Maybe that means waiting a little longer or saving up a little more. That just gives you more time to focus on your business idea, products/services and value.

Ten questions to ask potential web designers before you hire them

1. Can I have a list of five references that I can contact?

2. Do you do this full-time? How long have you been in business?

3. Who does the work? If it's not you, who are the employees, sub-contractors or outsourced people? How are they involved and how long have you worked with them?

4. What is your process?

5. What is the typical budget range for your projects?

6. What is the typical timeframe for your projects?

7. Can I have a list of 10-15 websites that you've built and what you were responsible for on them?

8. What is your process for updates and requests after the site is launched?

9. When are you available to start my project?

10. What would you need from me to start?

Getting an accurate project quote

Trying to get a price for your website can feel like an awkward dance.

"What do you charge?"

"It varies. What is your budget?"

"Well, I'm trying to get a sense of price so I can set my budget."

"Actually, in order to give you a quote, I need some idea of what you can spend."

"I won't know what to spend until I know what it costs…"

And so on, and so forth, until the music stops and you're both left in the middle of the dance floor, embracing each other awkwardly. This doesn't have to be the case, if both sides are upfront and honest from the start.

No web designer can give you a specific quote, right off the bat, without knowing the details of what you want. No two websites are exactly the same. They all have different features and factors that affect the price.

A better initial question would be to ask about the typical budget range, as I mentioned in the chapter titled *Finding the right web designer*. Since you've already got a budget for the project, you'll immediately know if it's possible to work together.

In order to get an exact quote, you'll need to give the web designer a lot of information about what you want your website to do. How do you know what your website should do? Refer back to your list of website goals. Think about each goal and what specific function the website needs to have in order to achieve that goal. If it's selling digital books, your website needs the ability to take people's money and give them a file (ecommerce). If a goal relates to building your audience through a newsletter, your website needs to capture names and email addresses into a mailing list and be able to send out emails.

If there are features you'd like your website to have that you'd simply love, but don't absolutely need, make a second list (a wants list) and get a separate price for those. This wants list can include things you think might help, future features you'd like your site to have, or stuff you're on the fence about. Know that it's better to launch with less and be more focused. The web is fluid and your website can be too—things can be added down the road when they make sense.

If you've got an existing website, that's a great starting place to figure out the project scope. What do you want to keep? What needs to change? To be added?

When listing the features you want, there's no need to be technical or even specific—just list what you'd like your website to do in plain English. For example, instead of saying, "I need to use 'X' WordPress plugin for my shopping cart that ties into PayPal and Mailchimp," you could say, "I need to be able to sell products and save purchaser information to a mailing list." This leaves room for your web designer to propose solutions that might be more effective or work better with the overall project.

Lean on your web designer to make suggestions about best practices, best software and best solutions—they live this and have deep expertise, since they build websites for a living. Plus, it gives you the chance to hear their logic and reasoning for proposed solutions, in order to assess if they really will work for you.

Five common features your website might need

1. Ecommerce - this can be anything from a 'Buy Now' PayPal button to a fully customized shopping cart. Be clear about how you envision your ecommerce working. What are you selling? Is it digital or physical? How does order fulfillment work?

2. Blog - will you have a blog or news section? Will there be categories? Tags? Comments? Photos for each post? Is it searchable?

3. Newsletter - what information do you need to collect from subscribers (just email, or more)? Will your list need to be segmented (by region, age, other)? Will there be more than one design for emails you send out? Will the emails have daily, weekly, or monthly frequency?

4. Social media - will there be a Facebook or Twitter feed? Thumbnails of recent Instagram photos?

5. Visuals - will there be slideshows? Embedded presentations or videos? Visualizations, animations or graphics that need to be created? Photo galleries or music players?

Typical information you need to give a web designer to get an accurate quote

1. What are the goals of my website?

2. What does my website need to do?

3. What is my budget and timeline?

4. What do I want new visitors to do when they come to my site? What do I want returning visitors to do (if it differs)?

5. What are the competing websites? What do I like/dislike about their sites? How am I different?

6. Do I need logo design? Print design? Other graphics?

7. What am I looking for? A fully functional website? Newsletter design and templating? E-commerce integration? Hosting/server setup? Email setup? Domain name setup?

Your project responsibilities

Building a website is a lot of work... for you. Before, during and after the project you'll have just as much on your plate as the professionals you've hired to help build it, so plan accordingly. Even with the best people on your team, you can't just look at a couple mockups, wait a few weeks and shout, "let's launch this baby!"

Before the project even starts, you'll need to have your shit together. Figure out what elements should go on each page. Make sure you have rough content planned for things like your tagline, sidebar, menu items and newsletter pitches (to name just a few). You'll also need to have a list of every service your web designer needs to access, along with the associated usernames and passwords.

During the project you have to be available (i.e. no three-week silent meditations in Taos) to quickly review everything you receive, or simply to answer questions. Your web designer made a promise to design and build your website in a reasonable amount of time, so you need to do what's required of you just as quickly.

Writing and editing content will probably be the biggest time consumer on your end. Web designers don't do this for you, and even if you hire a professional writer (which you should), your input will still be required. However long you think the content will take to complete, double it. That's at least how long it'll actually take—so plan to have enough time to do it. Almost every project I've ever done has been delayed because the content took longer than a client expected (even if I explained that from the start).

You also have to test your website to make sure everything works. Click every link, fill in every form, go through every process and proofread every sentence. It's your name and your ass on the line—so make sure everything is perfect before launch. No one wants their audience to be bug-checking their website instead buying things from it.

Clear (or greatly reduce) your schedule when your website project starts. That way you have time to do your job. Then you can actually reach the glorious next step, which is known as 'heck yes, launching!'

What your web designer needs before the project starts

1. Your style guide, if you've got one.

2. Your colour scheme, if you've got one.

3. Photography and graphics you'd like to use, in the highest resolution possible.

4. Your logo in vector format (ask whomever designed it for this file).

5. Access to all necessary services (including usernames and passwords) - hosting, domain registrar, newsletter, ecommerce, etc.

6. Your sitemap (this is a list of pages your site will have).

7. A list of 4-5 websites you like and why.

8. A list of 4-5 competing websites and what you like/dislike about them.

9. Your content, even if it's rough.

10. A list of what text or graphics should go in the header, footer and sidebar on every page.

Design tips

Here are some general guidelines to ponder before asking your web designer to create or change something in your website design.

Two to three colours are enough

A clown doesn't need to vomit rainbows onto a page for it to 'pop' (and don't ever use this word unless you're ordering a soda; it's not helpful in design because it isn't specific). Establish a couple brand colours. This will make your website feel like it has a consistent design language.

Two to three typefaces are enough

Just because millions of typefaces exist, it doesn't mean your website should use all of them, or even a dozen of your favourites. Just like a good colour palette, your site will have a stronger visual brand and more visual consistent language if you use just a few. As an added bonus, your content is far easier to read or scan quickly if it uses consistent colours and fonts.

Five to eight navigation items are enough

This is how visitors get from one page to another. Fewer menu items mean quicker scanning and finding. The page naming also needs to make sense, especially to first-time visitors. You can always use things like drop-down menus or even section-specific sidebar menus if absolutely necessary. Try a first draft of your menu and check with your web designer to ensure it makes sense from their perspective.

White space is not just for minimalists or art projects

The space between each element or section on your website gives your visual design enough room to breathe. It separates ideas and helps draw attention to the most important elements. If things are squished together or there's too much stuff on a page, it's hard to differentiate each individual element and equally tough for visitors to choose what they should actually do. There's elegance in simplicity, but more importantly, there are sound business reasons to focus on less. Too many options lead people to simply pick none of them (and probably to navigate away from your website in search of something clearer).

Minimalism can be bright, bold and colourful. It doesn't have to be stark white with muted, subtle tones. An effective minimal website could have a bright pink background (one colour, not 10) with white text in just two sizes (one for headings, one for paragraphs) that draw visitors to either read a blog entry or buy a product. This website would be very noticeable, but still have the minimal focus that encourages people to do just one or two things.

So before you ask your web designer to tighten up spacing or add more fonts, colours, patterns, anything—think about your audience. Will they be more likely to take action because you've used lots of fonts, or because your site is clear and focused?

People scroll... seriously, they scroll

Scientifically proven by Internet scientists (if they existed). Every usability study (these actually exist) has shown that people know what a scroll bar is and will in fact use it (even on mobile devices). The caveat is that they need a reason to scroll.

'The fold' is a mythical Internet ideal that was wrongly ported over from the print world (where things like newspapers actually 'fold'). The fold area (i.e. the amount of a website shown without scrolling) is different on every screen, browser and operating system. It's also very different on a mobile device or a tablet than on a huge desktop monitor.

Obviously, place important information higher up in the design. But focus more on making your content and design scroll-worthy. You have my promise (as a fake Internet scientist) that if you do, people will scroll to keep reading.

Standards exist for a reason

Your visitors shouldn't have to learn your website before they can use it. They won't, and instead, they'll just leave. While your style, brand and voice need to be creative, don't ever sacrifice understanding. Use clear language and visuals so they make sense to everyone. Keep items that appear on every page (like the logo and navigation) in the same place on each page so they're easier to find. Label pages and sections with words that make sense.

It's more important that visitors know how to do something than be wowed with your creative naming.

—

Your web designer knows a lot about what works and what doesn't in web design, since that's what they routinely get paid to do. There are reasons why most successful websites don't use every tool, font, colour or design element possible. Your site should be easy to use, so visitors can focus on what you're presenting to them, not the presentation itself.

Less is always more. Unless you're talking about focus—then I suppose more is more (and stop being a wise-ass, that's my job).

Critiquing mockups

No client assumes they know anything about web design until they're looking at a mockup they've paid for, which was designed by a professional. At that point they have a very strong opinion about what works online and what doesn't, what shade of blue is the best, how to correctly make something 'pop' or how to cram more information 'above the fold.' While your input as a client is completely valuable and even necessary, it needs to be framed and focused in the right ways.

Design is iterative and your web designer might not present you with a perfect mockup on the first try. This is good, because it can lead to a discussion about what problems still need solving, what's actually important as it relates to your goals, or something you might not have even considered. It's one thing to talk about your website in abstract terms and a very different thing to see it mocked up in front of you.

When giving your feedback, the most important thing to consider is that your site needs to serve your audience and goals, and not necessarily your own tastes. Your audience will be seeing, using and hopefully buying from your site. Put your personal views second.

Every design project is a beautiful balance between visual problem solving knowledge (from the designer) and knowledge of the audience and the business (from you). This is what makes every project different and keeps things interesting. So, rely on your web designer to propose the best visual solution. Before you start asking for changes, ask your designer some questions (and see the worksheet at the end of this chapter for all the questions you should ask yourself first).

Questions you might ask include: Why was the information designed in this way? Why was it placed where it is? Their answers and knowledge might convince you to keep something as-is.

If you aren't convinced by their pitch or the mockup, that's okay. You won't hurt their feelings if it's off the mark. This is a process. Be clear and specific about what you think isn't working, and frame it in a non-personal, non-insulting way. Web designers are used to change requests, but they can get defensive if you question their creative abilities (who wouldn't?).

Your change requests should also be actionable. Saying things like "punch that up a touch" or "dial the red back a hair" means absolutely nothing. Instead, say why something isn't working, such as, "that blue matches our direct competition so I'd rather use the orange from our logo instead," or "our style guide and logo have circular elements and everything in the mockup uses squares and hard lines, which doesn't match." Focus on what's not right or what problems still exist, instead of telling a web designer specifically how to fix things. They're professional problem solvers, so give them something to solve instead of a solution that might not be accurate.

If you ask for feedback from other parties (your spouse, your marketing department, your 'web designer' cousin)—know that they might not completely understand your online goals or the problems the design is solving (or at least not as much as the web designer). Take this feedback into consideration, but don't necessarily get your web designer to make all of the changes suggested.

Your web designer isn't your yes-person, either, so they might disagree with your change requests. This is actually a great thing, since it'll force you to evaluate what you've asked for and make a stronger case for the change. Disagreements happen, mostly because a good web designer is as passionate as you are about creating an awesome final product. You both want the same thing (a kick-ass finished product), so don't get personal, upset or offended. Your goals are the same—you're just working out the details.

Oh, and also always ask your web designer to make the logo bigger—we love that. Just think about how many times you used someone else's website and thought "I'd buy something here, but only if the logo was 10% larger."

Eleven questions to ask yourself about every design element before you make a change request

1. Does this help to accomplish my goals?
2. What's memorable about this, and could anything make it more memorable?
3. Who needs to see or know this information?
4. Why is this worth clicking?
5. Can this be simplified and still make sense?
6. Is this necessary?
7. What's the obvious next step?
8. Would it matter if a specific element was removed?
9. What problem does this solve for my audience?
10. Does this change someone's mind?
11. Is this exactly what I want to say, in the voice and tone I want to say it in?

Making your website credible

People will judge a book by its cover (instantly, too). If you're trying to sell or promote anything online, no one is going to buy or listen unless they feel they can trust you.

Trust and credibility aren't measured in absolutes and sometimes it's just a feeling (yes, I brought up feelings, and no, I'm still not singing *kumbaya*) that your website elicits when people see it for the first time.

Having a professionally designed website is definitely a brilliant first step on your part. It gives your business a cohesive visual language. But design is only one aspect of establishing trust.

The web design is as important as the photography, which is as important as the tone and content, which is as important as the actual offerings, which are as important as how the website actually works. If you do one of these things badly, the whole site can fall to pieces. Your credibility goes out the window if your site looks amazing but features poorly lit, MySpace-style self-portraits taken in your bathroom.

There are a few general guidelines that can help you establish trust (see the following worksheet). Your website needs to prove your expertise and its purpose before you can get anyone to sign up, read or buy anything. Your authority and knowledge must be instantly showcased.

You have a website because you have something to offer that you believe kicks serious ass—so make sure people know that when they view it.

Twelve ways to make your website more credible

1. Is my messaging clear, simple and honest? Does it make sense to first-time visitors?

2. Am I showcasing what others think of me through testimonials or reviews?

3. Is there evidence that my business exists elsewhere on the Internet (guest posts or reviews on other websites)?

4. Do I have any endorsements from industry authorities or a well-known source (i.e. I'm featured in O magazine)?

5. Do all my links work? Are my social media feeds working?

6. Do I give reasons for actionable items and not just 'click here' or 'buy now'?

7. Are there spelling or grammar mistakes?

8. Is my contact information easily found?

9. Do I have an email address @mycompanywebsite.com (and not a @gmail.com or @aol.com address)?

10. Does my site load quickly? Even on mobile devices?

11. Am I showcasing real-life examples or case studies that prove the benefits of what I'm offering?

12. Does my website look alive (with fresh blog posts, social media updates, new testimonials, etc.)?

Writing effective content

The design and functionality of your website, if done properly, should blend into the background and subconsciously make your brand shine, while promoting trust in what you do. Content, however, is very noticeable, since it has to be read and absorbed to be understood.

Definitely hire a professional to help. One thing that sets my most successful clients apart from other clients is that they've all hired good content writers or content strategists (even if clients are writers themselves).

Good content is right

Right for your brand, right for your business and its goals, and right for your audience. It needs to be appropriate and understandable. People reading it for the first time need to get it, and once someone has read it, they should feel compelled to act on it in some way (relating to your goals, hopefully).

What would your brand sound like if it could talk? The good news is that you are your brand. So use language that's genuine to how you communicate. The tone of your content should be easy to master because it's your authentic tone. When you're excited about your expertise, industry and offerings, that 'true stoke' will shine through.

Good content is quick

Say as much as possible while saying as little as possible, because online readers have the collective attention span of a gnat (not because they're dumb, but because they're bombarded with constant streams of information).

Just like in design, content minimalism is not an abstract ideal that works sometimes; it's a sound practice that works for each and every website. Say things quickly and get straight to the point. It's the most effective way to get your message across to people.

Good content is useful

Even if (or especially if) you're selling something—you need to explain how it solves a problem or provides value, over simply saying, "Click here to BUY NOW!!!" It won't even matter how many exclamation marks or capital letters you use. Offer benefits, results, reasons and usefulness in what you write.

Good content is consistently consistent

Before you write a single blog post, tagline, action item or newsletter—think about the tone and language of your brand. It all needs be consistent, which it will be if it fits your brand's style and tone. A professional can really help with this.

Have a style guide—even if it's in your head—that influences how you write copy. What language do you use, and in what way? If all your content sounds like it comes from the same clear voice, it'll feel like your brand, be more easily understood, and enhance your credibility.

Your content should also match your visual style. If your website's visuals are fun and 'pop' (just kidding), then your copy shouldn't read like it was written by a group of corporate accountants (sorry accountants!).

Good content is sharable

Think about the blog posts that you and everyone else in your online social circles share with followers. What do they have in common?

They're probably not pushy, hard to understand (due to technical language or esoteric metaphors) or in a format you don't like consuming (videos, photos, charts, and even blog posts don't appeal to everyone). They're probably written in the author's real voice, too, with an honest agenda that goes beyond simply making a sale. They probably resonate deeply with you, provide useful insight or even solve a common problem.

Good content is a story

Regardless of culture, human beings have a shared heritage of telling stories to pass along knowledge. People naturally connect with and appreciate a good story. Think about how you can weave a story around what you're trying to say, because stories are interesting, even if the subject matter is dry.

Good content is professionally done

You don't have to hire a writer to create all your website copy from scratch, but you should definitely hire someone to proofread, tweak, suggest changes or talk content strategy and tone with you. Everyone misses tone differences, typos or grammar-o's (probably not a word, but you know what I mean) in their own work. You might be too close or knowledgeable about your subject matter to effectively gauge whether it's easily understandable.

Even best-selling authors work with professionals to read and edit their work before it goes public. That's just a good idea and a sound business practice.

As I said in the first chapter, every successful site I've worked on that's been a success involved hiring a writing professional. Two sets of eyes are better than one (unless you're a cyclops or pirate, then possibly 1.5 sets of eyes are better than half a set).

—

You've got to write epic shit that sounds like your brand. There's no magical 'click here to go viral' button or service.

Just keep writing at the intersection of your skills and passions.

Ecommerce

To make money, you've got sell something on your website (file under: obviously). From services to digital products to things you have to package and ship, the premise is basically the same to take a potential customer from hearing about what you offer through to giving you money for it.

There are entire books written about how to effectively sell and create perfect ecommerce experiences for your audience. But really, it all boils down to a couple key points.

Establish trust

This first step is to ensure your website and brand look credible (see chapter titled *Making your website credible*). Next, people have to trust the payment process. Is it a service they've used before (like PayPal or Amazon Payments or Stripe)? If not, are there security indicators (such credit cards processed on an SSL page—your web designer will help with this) or digital certificates? Is there a visible return policy and clear contact information? Do you list shipping costs or provide shipping calculators for physical goods without getting halfway through the checkout process first?

Make the sale easy

Make an online purchase simple for a potential customer by using the least number of steps possible. Also, make sure the process is easy to understand, and doesn't collect information you don't need. If possible, stick to a single page with limited form fields to gather payment information (credit card number, expiry date and security code are required—everything else is nice to have), that doesn't require users to create an account before they make a purchase (unless it's absolutely necessary) and clearly list the answers to common questions people might ask before a purchase—including shipping fees, return policies or notices that an item is out of stock.

Keep in touch

Once someone has purchased something from you, keep the lines of communication open. That could include order confirmation emails, shipping/tracking notices, or introducing new and related offers. If someone has bought something from you once, they might be interested in buying more – if you treat them well. And if they've enjoyed what they bought, make sure it's easy for them to share that experience through reviews and social media platforms.

You should also save all customer email addresses to a mailing list (your web designer can set this up), so you can use an auto-responder to check in a week later and see if your buyers are enjoying their purchase.

Selling self-published products & services

Once your products are ready for sale, you've got to complete a few more steps before you can release them to the world for purchase.

If you've got a publisher, retailer, or anyone else who's taking care of your supply chain, your product (and its inventory) and payment processing, you're already set. If not, and if you're self-publishing digital or physical goods, you should create a few additional items that will maximize customer responses and prepare you for selling.

The offering

If you've created a physical product, focus on supply and inventory. You never want to sit on too much inventory, but you also don't want to run out of something that's selling well. So, there's a balance. You can always gauge initial interest in a new product by offering pre-sales before the official release.

If your product is digital, then you need to think about the best delivery format. A digital product can be anything from an ebook to a studio album to a spoken podcast to a video lecture series. Think about all the different ways your product will be used and consumed. For example, does it need to work on mobile devices? Does the format work on both Mac and PC platforms? What's the best quality you can offer in a downloadable size? Does the product need to live in multiple formats?

Ebooks could be in PDF, mobi, ePub or even a proprietary format like Apple's textbook. All these formats (except for PDF) can't be formatted or too design-heavy (which is why you're currently reading this book in PDF format).

Podcasts and music can be in MP3, WAV, AAC or a myriad of other compressed or lossless formats. MP3 tends to be the most widely useable format for audio.

For videos, you can either use private websites where buyers stream your content after entering a username or password, or by offering the video for download (typically in AVI, MP4 or MOV format).

To figure out what format works best for your product, look at similar products that sell well and take note of their delivery formats. There's probably a good reason that popular products are sold in their current format, or at least they've set a precedent that people can expect for other, similar products.

If you're selling a service (like coaching), it's never a bad idea to offer complementary products—such as a workbook file that people can write on and save, information sheets, a reference guide, or anything customers can go back to after they've consumed your service.

Free content

Giving away part of what you've created has become the norm for self-published digital work. If you give away the right portion of what you've created, you'll tease people into wanting the rest. A free sample is also a good way to give tentative potential customers a glimpse into what they'd receive if they paid for the full product. Once they invest time into the sample, they'll be more inclined to want the whole thing.

Free content could include:

1. The first two chapters of your ebook. The last page of the sample (and in the footer of every page) should include a link to buy the full book.

2. Two songs from your album. Include the album artwork and digital insert/booklet to show downloaders what they're missing if they don't buy the whole thing.

3. A video introduction to your video series. This shows people the style they'd receive, as well as the personality and flavour of the paid-for videos.

Sales page

Possibly the most important product sales or service piece is the page that describes what's for sale and offers a clear way for people to buy it.

Lately, the norm seems to be these super long-form sales pages that seem to scroll forever (yes people scroll, but if it's 20 pages of testimonials, it's easier to close the page than to keep reading). If you can't show a potential customer why they should want what you've got in a sentence or two, you haven't clearly defined the value of your offering.

Be clear, concise and make it all about your buyers. How will they benefit? Why should they want to pay for it? How will it enrich or better their lives? Will they want to tell everyone they know how awesome it is? Focus on that—in as few words as possible.

Testimonials are also a great way to build credibility, especially if they come from someone your potential customers recognize. Before you launch your product, contact several people in your industry or from similar fields that your audience respects, and see if they would like a free copy of what you'll be selling. And if they dig it, ask if they wouldn't mind writing you a short testimonial.

Payment processing and delivery

To collect money from online buyers, you need a way to process a credit card. This can happen on your website or through a payment processor's website (like PayPal, Stripe or Amazon Payments). The latter tends to be cheaper, but pulls customers away from your site to enter their financial information at a secure location. This isn't necessarily a bad thing, as many of these processor companies let you add your logo to the top of the payment page and direct folks back to your site once their card is processed. To process a credit card on your own site, you need to ensure your site is absolutely secure, completely reliable and totally trustworthy.

A physical product should ship within 24 hours after a purchase. A digital product should be delivered immediately after purchase—which typically means sending your buyer an automated email with a download link that enables them to pick up a copy of what they bought.

Additional distribution

Just because you're self-publishing a digital product doesn't mean it can't be distributed to bigger websites that many people frequent. If you've got a book or music, it's easy to list it on Amazon or iTunes through any digital distributor (CD Baby and BookBaby – which are owned by the same company – are good examples of music and book distributors for indie creators). There's no harm in selling your product on your own website, as well as listing it in bigger online stores. The more places it shows up, the more likely the right people are to see it. Most independent content distributors don't charge a whole lot for their services, either.

Media and affiliate information

Whatever you're selling, make sure to provide easy-to-find information to help people promote your product. You can also make it worth their while by offering a cut of the profits through an affiliate program, which is a profit-share between you and someone else promoting your product.

If someone wants to share your offering with others, for the love of social media gurus, make sure it's easy for them to do so. Provide digital promotion badges for use on their websites, contact information for interviews, social media sharing prompts, copy-and-paste-able product descriptions and even a short bio, if that's applicable.

Self-publishing checklist

- ✓ Is my product in the best format for my buyers? Should it be offered in multiple formats?

- ✓ Is there a free sample available? Does it include obvious links to purchase?

- ✓ Have I collected at least a handful of testimonials for the sales page?

- ✓ Is physical distribution required? If so, have I set that up?

- ✓ Have I tested the ecommerce process?

- ✓ Have I connected my mailing list with the ecommerce process (your web designer can help with this step)?

- ✓ Have I set up an automated email about a week after purchase to see if someone liked my product and wants to share it with others?

- ✓ Is it easy for people to share my product with others on social media? Do I have images that can be pinned on Pinterest? Short blurbs that can be tweeted? Compelling suggestions for text and images that can be quickly posted to Facebook?

Your launch responsibilities

You're relying on the professionals you've hired to make your website, so you've got to do your part if you ever want to launch it.

There are actually quite a few things you'll need to do during a web project. Clarifying your goals, answering questions, reviewing mockups and writing content all need your attention and time.

You've got to set a launch date (after you've talked with the professionals involved to see if it's realistic). Stick to it by delivering your work on time or before it's due. Create a list with your web designer outlining your respective responsibilities and when they're due. It will keep you both accountable and acts as a to-do list, so when you finish one thing, you know what's next and what's left.

In addition to content, if your website has a blog, you need to have at least a handful of blog posts written and ready for launch. This will give visitors a sense of what to expect, where your authority lies, and a reason to subscribe or to come back for more.

If you're new to social media, you need to make sure your accounts are set up and active prior to launch. Start building a following, then tease details about the launch and interact with the type of people you think might be interested in what you have to offer. If you're already using social media, it's a good idea to announce your launch date—it gives people an expected timeframe, and it keeps you accountable (since everything you write on the Internet has to be true).

Your online business and presence is more than just your website. It's social media, newsletters, statistics, feeds, and possibly a lot more. You have to make sure everything that connects to or from your website is working.

On launch day, confirm with your web designer when your site is actually live and ready to share with the world. When it launches, tell your friends, colleagues, family, followers, everyone. Offer discounts or freebies, incentives to sign up or follow you, or even just something ephemeral and fun to celebrate the launch (perhaps it's a video of you singing *kumbaya*).

Make sure you keep track of your supporters and ad-hoc marketing team (i.e. anyone who promotes your new website) so you can thank them personally.

Finally, doing a little launch day dance will make your site load faster. You should celebrate—launching is a huge accomplishment.

Pre-launch checklist

- ✓ Have I proofread everything?

- ✓ Have I tested every link, click, feature, process, and form on my website?

- ✓ Are all my social media entities connected?

- ✓ Is my mailing list collecting email addresses (sign up to test)? Do I have a branded template in place for sending out emails?

- ✓ Is there a statistics program tracking visitors?

- ✓ Do I have a plan to generate buzz and excitement for launch day?

- ✓ Is there a website backup plan in place to save my files and content?

- ✓ Do I have strong passwords for website admin access that can't be guessed?

- ✓ Do all of my social media accounts look like my new website? Are the photos the same? Is the bio the same? The URL correct?

- ✓ Am I available on launch day to work on, fix or change anything that might need to be done on my end?

Post-launch responsibilities

The launch of your website is only the start of your online business. You can't just launch and watch sales roll in (although that'd be nice if it happened—money fight on the yacht!).

Now you've got to hustle, promote and market. Write blog posts showcasing your expertise, provide real value, and keep writing. Connect and engage on social media. Release new product offerings or updates.

People can tell if a website has gone stale, and no one wants to buy from one that doesn't feel current anymore. Was your blog last updated when grunge music was cool? Or worse, is your last blog post a year old and an apology for not blogging for the last few years? Does your Twitter feed have one (and only one) tweet saying that your new website is live? Are there unanswered questions in the comments section of your blog posts? Have folks forgotten they're on your mailing list because you haven't ever sent out an email?

All of these things make you look bad. Like you don't care enough about your website to keep it updated or put time into it. It's a smart practice (and I know you're a smart cookie) to keep things rolling with new ideas, value, content, products, updates, and things that keep your audience engaged and wanting to come back for more. Add new case studies or even reviews/testimonials as they come in, and create new products/services as old ones run their course.

You need a maintenance plan for your website. You should also talk to your web designer about automating off-site backups for both your content and files. There's nothing worse than a hacked website, a server that's gone kaput, or getting infected with malware and having to start from scratch as the only option. It's ridiculous not to invest in regular backups—servers are so cheap, and the whole thing can easily be automated.

Post-launch checklist

- ✓ Keep blogging, keep using social media, keep sending out newsletters.

- ✓ Have automated backups in place and a schedule for my website's software updates.

- ✓ Check my stats. See who's linking to my website and what content they're linking to.

- ✓ Monitor and respond to feedback - blog comments, mentions, Facebook conversations, emails.

- ✓ Is my website's URL in my email signature, on my social media profiles and on my business cards? Does it make sense to also link to my latest blog post in my email signature?

- ✓ Is it time to create a new product, service or offering?

- ✓ Is my website reaching my business goals? If not, why not and how can I change/adjust? If it is achieving my goals, do I need new or bigger goals?

Website maintenance schedule

Daily

- ✓ Check email, check comments and check social media mentions/conversations.
- ✓ Monitor website traffic. Where are people coming from? What pages are they visiting? What pages are they leaving from? Are there error pages?
- ✓ Engage with people on social media.

Weekly

- ✓ Write a blog post (or two). Promote them on social media.
- ✓ Send an email to your newsletter subscribers (it can be related to the blog post).
- ✓ Review who's talking about your online business and where they're talking about it.
- ✓ What's currently popular on your website? What content gets the most reaction or sharing on social media? How can you do more of that?

Website maintenance schedule (continued)

Monthly

- ✓ Evaluate your goals. Are you reaching them? Do they need to be adjusted/altered?

- ✓ Gauge your audience's interests. How can your online business serve that interest?

- ✓ Where does your audience spend their time online? Can you offer value there? Think about writing guest posts, comments, and answering their questions.

Yearly

- ✓ Evaluate your goals. Are you reaching them? Do they need to be adjusted/altered?

- ✓ Survey your existing customers or visitors. How can you serve them better?

- ✓ Is it time for a new offering, product or service?

- ✓ Do you need to renew your domain name?

- ✓ Does your hosting, newsletter program and ecommerce system serve your needs?

- ✓ How can you keep your existing audience interested and engaged?

Promoting your website

Possibly the question I hear most often is "How do I get people to my website?" Everyone wants their work to be read, shared and valued—and in order to do that, the right kind of people have to find it first.

To build an audience, you first need to figure out where they spend their time online. What sites do they frequent? What forums do they use? What products/services do they currently consume? Who do they follow and interact with on social media?

On a one-to-one scale, this is sometimes called 'stalking' (which seems negative and creepy). On a business scale, this can be called 'research' (which sounds important and necessary). You can find this out through polling (even informally by asking a question on social media) or by looking at similar websites and seeing who's commenting on posts or tweeting to them. You can also ask people you know are (or would be) your audience the questions in the previous paragraph.

This research will lead you to a list of websites and people that your desired audience already follows. Interact with people on these websites, leave comments on blog posts they're reading, interact with them on the social media network they're using the most often, and join their active communities.

Your goal shouldn't be sales, but instead, to provide value, assistance and insight. Offer advice, opinions and expertise. There's always a link back to your website (in comments, profiles or in your profile on social media). Think of it like this —it's not what you can get from your audience; it's what value you can bring to them. It's the best way to net a more engaged and lasting audience for your online business.

You can also write content for others (in the form of guest blogging or videos, or submitting articles to online magazines) and give some of your knowledge away for free. Guest posts enhance your authority in your field and ensure the content you write is read by a larger group of people than you might otherwise be able to reach. Get in touch with websites that offer guest writing and pitch the value you can bring to their readers.

You can also have guest posts or even interviews on your own website (since the person you're interviewing will promote the post). Spotlight people who can bring value and knowledge to your audience, and everyone wins.

The web isn't just blog posts—it's videos, PDFs, audio, short pieces of inspiration, long essays, Facebook posts, Instagram photos and many more types of content. What does your audience like to consume? Do more of that. If you aren't sure, see what they're sharing most often, or simply ask them (that's always easiest).

Once you've drawn someone to your website (congrats on that, by the way), you need to make damn sure they know what to do next. After every blog post you've written, there should be a prominent next step. Is it signing up for your newsletter? Checking out your latest product? Following you on Twitter? Pick what benefits your online goals the most, and go with that. Just don't include a huge list of next steps at the bottom of every blog post, or your readers will lose focus and click away from your site.

Check your statistics and see what content gets the most links and page views. Promote that content and if applicable, write similar content. Hell, add a popular posts widget in your sidebar to promote posts that are proven to provide the most value.

You don't have to be an Internet scientist to measure the results of your online business efforts. Set yourself up for success by writing at least a handful of blog posts each month (consistency builds traffic). This shows you care enough about your website to put real work into it. Then look at how many people took action after reading each post (by sharing on social media, commenting, signing up for your newsletter or buying your product). Use your statistics to see how many inbound links (i.e. websites that link to you) your blog posts receive. If those two things are tiny or non-existent, it might be time to rethink your strategy or the content of your blog posts. Maybe it's even time to switch up the format (change your written posts to video blogs, for example). Perhaps your action items at the end of each post aren't actionable enough. Posts that ask readers a question at the end of the post tend to get more comments, for example.

Business has always been about building relationships, and online business is the same. So make sure to connect with like-minded folks and businesses that offer similar services or reach similar audiences. Actually talk to people without trying to sell them something or use their audience to your advantage. That doesn't work in the real world (or at least it seems sort of slimy), and it doesn't fly online. Share ideas, connect and offer to actually help others. Talk to your audience like you'd talk to a friend. People see through insincerity, but they also value genuine connections. And that's just good business.

Focus less on building numbers (like followers or stats or mailing list subscribers). These numbers are vapid and ephemeral, because they don't accurately gauge your real and lasting audience. Instead, foster relationships, engagement and provide value to people who will truly benefit from what you have to offer. Personally, I'd rather see 100 people using my Facebook page (if I used Facebook) get so stoked about my next book that they shout it from the rooftop (or on social media—which is probably more effective), than 10,000 likers who've never been to my website or clicked on a single article I've posted.

When you're promoting your business and what it offers online, there needs to be a reason for your work. 'Buy now' or 'click here' are not reasons, any more than someone yelling, "hey you, buy this vacuum!" on the street is a good strategy (unless, I suppose, you were on the street looking for good deals on vacuums from strangers). Remember, you're focused on bringing value to others, and that value should be more present than anything else you're promoting.

Be different, be valuable, be awesome. Because you are. You've built something you're totally stoked about and your online business helps others in some way. Let that shine through, and you're set.

Building a newsletter

A newsletter is possibly the most powerful and effective way to reach your audience; because you're arriving them right in their inboxes. It forces consumption; since most people see every email they receive (and might not read every tweet from every follower they have or visit your website every day). A newsletter gives you a tremendous amount of power, so use it wisely.

First, you need to build your subscriber list. That means giving people a reason to sign up for your newsletter. Are you prepared to offer something useful for subscribing—i.e. a freebie, part of the ebook you sell, discounts for other products, newsletter-only content? Even more importantly, can you give them a clear reason why your newsletter will be consistently valuable?

Your newsletter signup form needs to be prominent and actually look like a signup form. It's also not a bad idea to mention how often you'll show up in their inbox, especially if it's more than once a week. If you're emailing them daily, be sure that's totally clear before they sign up. And if that's the case, try to offer additional options, like weekly or monthly digests.

Now that you've got a list of subscribers, make sure the content of each newsletter has the right tone—a voice that matches your website. Encourage people to reply to you, so you're creating more of a conversation and less of a one-way speech.

Just like blog post action items, if you want your readers to do something after they read the email, focus on a single action—like buying a product, reading the full blog entry, or sharing it on social media. One actionable item per email keeps the focus clear and will net the best results.

There's no reason a newsletter shouldn't be part of your online business plan. Growing a subscriber list that you actively engage with newsletters is a great way to reach your audience exactly where they are. Keep them interested, since you'll lose them forever if they click 'unsubscribe.' Stay true to your voice, stay engaging and most of all, stay valuable.

Using social media

Putting sharing buttons on each blog post is not a social media strategy. You have to actually engage with your audience and offer unique value on social media (but it doesn't always have to be about selling). Plus, your content needs to resonate with people if you're hoping they'll share it.

There aren't enough hours in the day to use every single social media network, even if that was your full-time job. Figure out where your ideal audience hangs out and start by using those networks.

Actually connect with people. Reply to things they say, offer answers if they ask questions, share valuable content that they write, and create relationships. Don't always make it about selling or promoting yourself. Be real on social media, instead of trying to act like a professional company. Being true to yourself instead of sounding like a PR robot is a good thing, whether you work for yourself or have a staff of 500. We all relate to people more than a lifeless corporation that speaks marketingese.

Don't be afraid to just be yourself. First off, it's easy to do, since you're normally yourself. Secondly, your brand and its tone will be more relatable if you are natural.

You've also got to adapt quickly to change, since social media and its norms can change fast. Just because something worked last week, doesn't mean it'll work again now. Your audience might all jump ship on one network and join another (remember when everyone back in the early days used ICQ to chat online and now no one uses ICQ?). Stay up to date with how and where your audience spends their time socializing online.

Obviously, you've also got to stand out. You want to have your content shared and discussed (hopefully in a positive way). So what can you offer your audience on social media that achieves that goal? What unique value do you bring to each conversation? It's all about relationships, and relationships aren't built by shouting marketing slogans at people or continually sharing other people's content, or simply using your space on social media as a feed for a different social media network (i.e. using your Twitter feed to simply repost Pinterest photos, or your Facebook feed to post your tweets).

Effective social media usage is more about relationships than selling, so be generous, genuine and engaging with your audience.

Conclusion

If I could sum the whole book up with a few main points, they'd be:

1. Have clear goals for your online business.

2. Always hire professionals.

3. Be yourself.

4. Know how much work is involved for all parties.

5. Continually make an effort to be relevant and valuable to your audience.

6. You can do this.

Never be afraid to ask questions of the people you hire—there are no dumb questions, nor are you a bad client for asking (unless you're asking to make the logo bigger or to make something 'pop'). The people you've hired have done more projects like this than you have, since they do it for a living. So, the onus is on them to teach you or provide you with answers. If they aren't happy to provide you with answers, they're not doing their jobs properly.

There's obviously no specific formula for online success. This book will hopefully help to guide you, and the worksheets are there for quick reference. If it was easy, every single person who ever built a website would be having money fights on their private yachts (even in the heyday of the Internet, this rarely happened).

If you focus on bringing value to others instead of trying to sell to them, you'll be way ahead of the game.

Starting and running a business is hard but rewarding work. The Internet has made it possible to run things from practically anywhere. We are in a unique time where ideas, products, services can be spread without buy-in or promotion from large, traditional media outlets or huge publicity companies. With the right knowledge and tools in place, you can succeed and be satisfied on levels that go far beyond the financial.

So now, it's time for you to *crush it*.

Companion book

Create awesome content,

Cheri Hanson

Create awesome content is a straightforward guide to attracting and engaging your audience. You'll learn how to develop a simple content strategy, write top-notch copy, and how to work with a writer or content creator if you get the sweats when your hands hit the keyboard (no judgement).

Author Cheri Hanson demystifies everything from online storytelling to the difference between active and passive voice. English class was never this much fun -- or this valuable. In today's hyper-connected digital world, everyone needs awesome content to stand out from the crowd. Get the inside scoop on how to create kick-ass web copy, articles, newsletters, blogs and more in this practical and entertaining ebook.

cherihanson.com/books/awesome-content

Resources

Here are some third-party services that my clients and I use on a regular basis to build and easily maintain websites, and to promote them properly.

I wasn't paid to suggest any of these services nor do I make money from these recommendations—I just actually like these companies and trust what they do.

The one exception is PayPal, who I fucking hate, but at the time I wrote this, they are still the industry standard for cheap credit card processing and for the most part, their service works and integrates with other necessary things.

These are the services that personally work for me, however, each project is a unique snowflake. Talk to your web designer to see what will work for your project.

Newsletter

A newsletter is a key part of attracting and interacting with your audience. I suggest MailChimp.com for your newsletter or for RSS-to-Email.

Statistics

To see how many people have visited your site, what pages they've clicked on and where they came from, you need to stay on top of your website statistics. I suggest Google Analytics, or for a quick snapshot, JetPack by WordPress. Both are free.

Payment processing

If you're going to sell digital products, like ebooks, videos, music, etc., you need a way to process credit cards and automatically deliver the files. I suggest PayPal and Sellfy.com, respectively. Sellfy is an amazing service that automatically delivers (via email) a secure link to your digital product after someone purchases it. And unlike PayPal, Sellfy consistently does a great job and has stellar support. Sellfy integrates with PayPal and Stripe.

Domain registration

A domain name is the website address or URL that people type into a browser reach your website, such as www.example.com. In order to get a domain name, you need to register one through a domain registrar. This is different than web hosting, although some companies provide both services. I suggest iwantmyname.com for domain registration (or failing that, anyone BUT GoDaddy—they're misogynistic, unethical assholes and their services are slow and painful to use).

Content Management

You need to be able to quickly create and edit the content on your website, which happens through something called a Content Management System (CMS for short). I suggest WordPress.org for your CMS. You can get a free website and pick your own theme from WordPress.com. Or, your web designer can get a self-hosted copy of WordPress from wordpress.org and design a custom theme for you.

Distribution

For some digital products you create, like books or music, there are companies that will get your independently made work into large online stores such as Amazon or iTunes. I've always gone with CD Baby for music and BookBaby for writing (they're the same cool company). Just upload your product and they distribute it to the major places where people buy similar digital products. Neither service costs very much ($50/album and $100/book).

About the author

Paul Jarvis has created websites for awesome people since the 90s. His clients know him as a straight-shooting, no-bullshit sort of fellow. All of them are references too—because he always does great work and always keeps the business goals in mind.

He's a practicing yogi, touring musician, a non-preachy vegan (yes they exist) and has a tattoo (or two). He currently lives in the woods, on an island with his wife Lisa and pet rats Ohna' and Awe:ri.

Thanks

Lisa (my wife) for putting up with everything that came after, "Hey, I'm going to write another book…" as well as copyediting the shit out this once it was finished. She also made me look good in the photo on the *About* page.

Cheri Hanson for editing this book (and everything else I publish) and being my sounding board for every crazy idea I had about writing a business book with lots of swearing and hippy song references.

Dyana Valentine for clarity and guidance. Marc Ensign, who I blatantly ripped off for the first line of the book. Also: Abby Kerr, Anna Brones, Danielle LaPorte, Matt Cheuvront, Natalie Rousseau (Horscroft) and Angie Wheeler for extreme awesomeness.

All of my clients. I'm fortunate enough to have worked with lots of extremely smart people who I've learned a great deal from. Without them, this book (and my career) would not be possible.

And you, the reader.

I appreciate that you've taken the time to read this book.

If you have any questions, want to do an interview or just want to talk about anything I've written, send me an email, paul@pjrvs.com.

If you found value in my words, please write a review on your website/blog, tell your friends to buy a copy, or let your social media followers know how it might be of value to them.

Stay awesome,
Paul Jarvis

Printed in Great Britain
by Amazon.co.uk, Ltd.,
Marston Gate.